Vocal Score from Annie

MIKE NICHOLS
Presents
A New Broadway Musical

Annie

Produced by
IRWIN MEYER   STEPHEN R. FRIEDMAN   LEWIS ALLEN

Lyrics by   Music by   Book by
MARTIN CHARNIN   CHARLES STROUSE   THOMAS MEEHAN

Starring

ANDREA   REID
McARDLE   SHELTON
SANDY   ROBERT
FAISON   FITCH

And

DOROTHY LOUDON

With
RAYMOND THORNE   LAURIE BEECHMAN

Settings by   Costumes by   Lighting by
DAVID MITCHELL   THEONI V. ALDREDGE   JUDY RASMUSON

Musical Direction and   Orchestrations   Production
Dance Music Arranged by   by   Stage Manager
PETER HOWARD   PHILIP J. LANG   JANET BEROZA

Musical Numbers Choreographed by
PETER GENNARO

Entire Production Directed by
MARTIN CHARNIN

Based on LITTLE ORPHAN ANNIE,®
by Permission of Chicago Tribune - New York News Syndicate, Inc.

Produced in Association with PETER CRANE

Originally Produced by the Goodspeed Opera House
MICHAEL P. PRICE, Executive Producer

ISBN 0-634-05782-0

HAL•LEONARD®
CORPORATION

7777 W. BLUEMOUND RD. P.O. BOX 13819 MILWAUKEE, WI 53213

In Australia Contact:
Hal Leonard Australia Pty. Ltd.
22 Taunton Drive P.O. Box 5130
Cheltenham East, 3192 Victoria, Australia
Email: ausadmin@halleonard.com

Visit Hal Leonard Online at
www.halleonard.com

CAST OF CHARACTERS
(in order of appearance)

Molly . . . . Danielle Brisebois
Pepper . . . . Robyn Finn
Duffy . . . . Donna Graham
July . . . . Kathy-Jo Kelly
Tessie . . . . Diana Barrows
Kate . . . . Shelley Bruce
Annie . . . . Andrea McArdle
Miss Hannigan . . . . Dorothy Loudon
Bundles McCloskey . . . . James Hosbein
Dog Catchers . . . . Steven Boockvor, Donald Craig
Sandy . . . . Himself
Lt. Ward . . . . Richard Ensslen
Sophie, the Kettle . . . . Laurie Beechman
Grace Farrell . . . . Sandy Faison
Drake . . . . Edwin Bordo
Mrs. Pugh . . . . Edie Cowan
Cecille . . . . Laurie Beechman
Annette . . . . Penny Worth
Oliver Warbucks . . . . Reid Shelton
A Star To Be . . . . Laurie Beechman
Rooster Hannigan . . . . Robert Fitch
Lily . . . . Barbara Erwin
Bert Healy . . . . Donald Craig
Fred McCracken . . . . Bob Freschi
Jimmy Johnson . . . . Steven Boockvor
Sound Effects Man . . . . James Hosbein
Bonnie Boylan . . . . Laurie Beechman
Connie Boylan . . . . Edie Cowan
Ronnie Boylan . . . . Penny Worth
NBC Page . . . . Mari McMinn
Kaltenborn's Voice . . . . Donald Craig
FDR . . . . Raymond Thorne
Ickes . . . . James Hosbein
Howe . . . . Bob Freschi
Morgenthau . . . . Richard Ensslen
Hull . . . . Donald Craig
Perkins . . . . Laurie Beechman
Honor Guard . . . . Steven Boockvor
Justice Brandeis . . . . Richard Ensslen

SCENES

ACT I
December 11 - 19, 1933

Scene 1:
The New York Municipal Orphanage (Girls' Annex)

Scene 2:
St. Mark's Place

Scene 3:
A Hooverville Under The 59th Street Bridge

Scene 4:
The Orphanage

Scene 5:
The Warbucks Mansion at Fifth Avenue and 82nd Street

Scene 6:
New York City

Scene 7:
The Orphanage

Scene 8:
Warbucks' Study

ACT II
December 21 - 25, 1933

Scene 1:
**The NBC Radio Studio at 30 Rockefeller Center
and the Orphange**

Scene 2:
The Orphanage

Scene 3:
Washington: The White House

Scene 4:
The Great Hall at the Warbucks Mansion

Scene 5:
The East Ballroom of the Warbucks Mansion

Applications for performance of this work, whether legitimate, stock amateur, or foreign, should be addressed to:

MUSIC THEATRE INTERNATIONAL
421 W. 54th St.
New York, NY 10019
Phone (212) 541-4MTI
Fax (212) FX7-4MTI

MUSICAL NUMBERS

OVERTURE

Lyric by MARTIN CHARNIN
Music by CHARLES STROUSE

Moderato (in 4)

IT'S THE HARD-KNOCK LIFE

Allegro (in 4) ♩ = 80

8

YOU'RE NEVER FULLY DRESSED
31 **WITHOUT A SMILE**

WE'D LIKE TO THANK YOU HERBERT HOOVER

TOMORROW

Slowly (in 4)

No. 2

ON CURTAIN

MAYBE

Slowly (in 4)

ANNIE: "Somewhere, somewhere"

Cls.

Cello

29 ANNIE (Vln. cola voce)

May - be far a - way, or may - be real near - by,

pizz.

he may be pour-ing her cof - fee, She may be straight-ning his tie.

37

May - be in a house all hid - den by a hill,

Bells

She's sit-ting play-ing pi - a - no, He's sit-ting pay-ing a bill.

+Brass

Bet - cha they're young, Bet - cha they're smart, Bet they col-lect____ things like

ash - trays and art.____ Bet-cha they're good,____ (why should-n't they be?)____

Their one mis-take was giv-ing up me.____ So,

last one of its kind; won't you please come get your "ba - by"

ALL CHILDREN:
May - be.

Vln. solo

Tutti

No. 2a

ANNIE'S ESCAPE

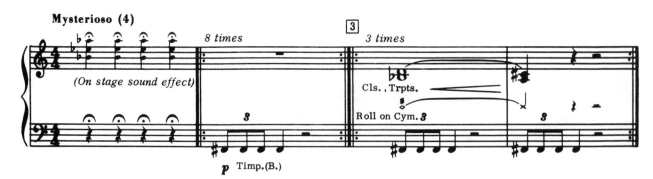

Mysterioso (4)

8 times

3 times

(On stage sound effect)

Cls., Trpts.

Roll on Cym.

Timp.(B.)

3 times

3 times

No. 2b

H. K. L. INTRO

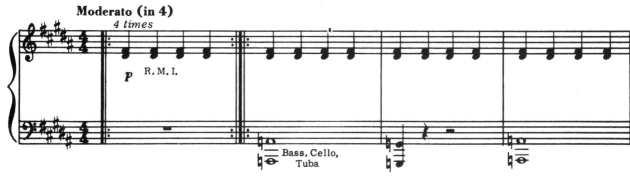

No. 3

IT'S THE HARD-KNOCK LIFE

22

seem like there's nev-er an-y light? Once a day don't you want to throw the

DUFFY & JULY:

towel in?___ It's eas-i-er than put-tin' up a **fight.** No one's

NELLY & PEPPER:

ANNIE:

+ Cls.

(Orphans:) Ooo _____ Ooo ___

there when your dreams at night get creep-y,___ No one cares if you grow or if you

Full of sor-row life!   No to--mor-row life!

Stgs.
Bells **p**

MOLLY: **49** +Fl. 8va   ANNIE:

San-ta Claus we nev - er see,   San - ta Claus what's that? Who's he?
p

Fl. 8va
Cls. **mf**

ALL:

No one cares for you   a smidge   when you're in an   or - phan-age!
mf

mf

"Shines like the top of
the Chrysler Building"

No. 3a

HARD-KNOCK LIFE REPRISE

SEGUE

No. 4

TOMORROW

WARD: "Now get along-cold in this weather"
VAMP   *50+51*   52

ANNIE: When I'm stuck with a   day   that's gray and

Last time only   Stgs.

lone-ly,___ I just stick out my   chin   and grin   and say:___   Oh, the

55+56

f

57

sun-'ll come out___ to-mor-row,   So ya got-ta hang on 'til to - mor-row___ come what

may! To - mor-row, to-mor-row, I love ya to-mor-row, you're

Br.

al - ways a day a - way! To - mor-row, to-mor-row, I

love ya to-mor-row you're al-ways a day a -

Tutti

way!

Trpts.

rall.

Timp.

No. 5

HOOVERVILLE

FRED: "we made Collier's again."

To-day we're liv-ing in a shan-ty, To-day we're scroung-ing for a

meal, To-day I'm steal-ing coal for fi - res, who knew I could

steal? I used to win-ter in the tro-pics, I spent my sum-mers at the

36

two in this blue heav-en___ that you__ gave us___ yes! We're turn-ing

blue! They of-fered us Al Smith and Hoo-ver, we paid at-ten-tion and we

chose not on-ly did we pay at-ten-tion, we paid through the

nose. In ev-'ry pot he said "a chick-en" But Her-bert Hoo-ver he for-

got!   Not on - ly don't we have the chick - en,   we   ain't got the

pot! Hey, Her - bie,   you left be - hind a grate - ful na - tion

ALL:
So Herb, our hats are off to you,   we're up to here with ad - mi - ra - tion,

SOPHIE:
come down and have a lit - tle stew.   Come down and have some Christ-mas

din - ner, Be sure to bring the Mis - sus too, we got no tur-key___ for our___ stuf-fin'___ why don't we stuff you.

Hoo - ver we'd like to thank you, Her-bert Thank you, Her - bie For real-ly show-ing us the way.

You dir - ty rat, you___ bu - reau - crat, you___ made us what we are to -

APPLAUSE SEGUE

No. 5a

INTRO HOOVERVILLE RAID

SEGUE AS ONE

No. 5b

HOOVERVILLE RAID

SEGUE AS ONE

No. 5c

BEFORE LITTLE GIRLS

Opening Scene 4

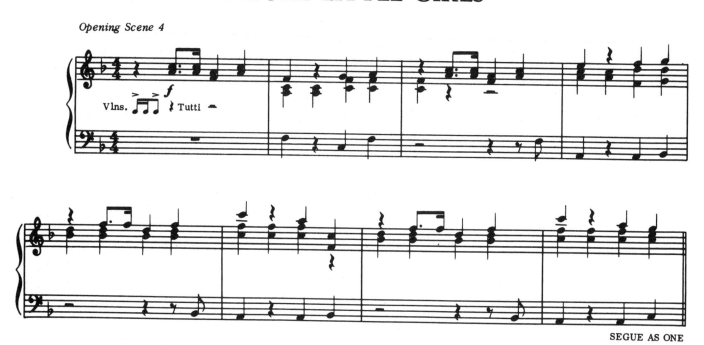

SEGUE AS ONE

No. 6

LITTLE GIRLS

As desk approaches

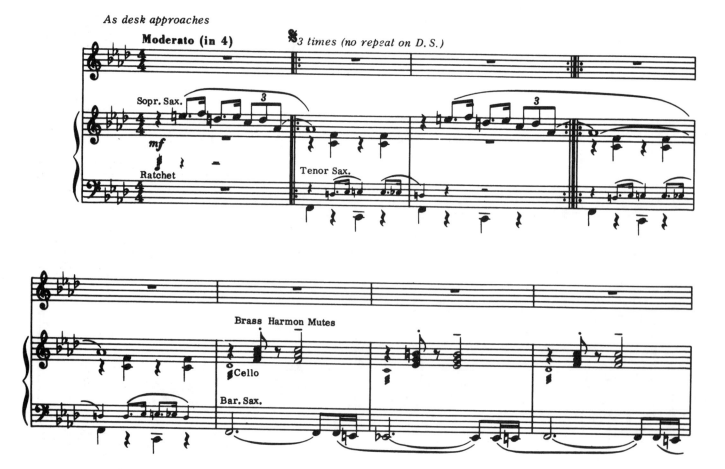

Luck-y me! Luck-y me! Look at what I'm drip-ping with lit - tle girls.

Sop. Sax.

Ten. Sax.

Cello
Bar. Sax.

MISS
HANNIGAN: "Shut up!"

How I hate lit-tle shoes, lit-tle socks and each lit-tle bloom-er.___
Safety

Brass

Alto Sax.

I'd have cracked years a-go if it weren't for my sense of hu - mor___

Brass
8va

62

Some-day I'll step on their freck-les, Some night I'll straight-en their curls

Saxs.

66

Send a flood, send the flu, an-y-thing that you can do to lit

Xylo.

Tutti

- tle girls.

cresc.

ff

Miss Hannigan
sits down!

sfz

No. 6a

LITTLE GIRLS REPRISE

MISS HANNIGAN "Get away, get away"

Alto Sax.

f

MISS HANNIGAN

Some day I'll land in the nut-house with all the nuts, and the squirrels.

Saxes

There I'll stay, tucked a-way til the pro-hib-i-tion of lit-tle girls.

Brass

SEGUE

No. 7

I THINK I'M GONNA LIKE IT HERE

An - nette comes in to make your bed.
Have an in - struc - tor here at noon.

ANNIE:
I think I'm gon - na like it here!
I think I'm gon - na like it here!
Brass

GRACE:
When you wake ring for Drake, Drake will bring your tray.
Pizz. Ww.
Cello

When you're through Mis - sus Pugh comes to take it a - way.

No. 8

N. Y. C.

lan - guage far from pure, e - nough of frank - furt - ers an - swer-ing back. __

etc.

Broth er, you know you're in N. Y. C.,

too bus - y, too cra - zy, too hot, too cold;

pizz.

Ww.

too late, I'm sold a - gain on N.

Tbn.

three bucks,   two bags,   one me.

155
N.   Y.   C.   I give you fair morn - ing

up there   in lights   I'll   be.   Go ask the

Brass

163
Saxs. cola voce
Gersh - wins   or Kauf-man and Hart   The place they love the   beat.   Tho' Cal-i-

Trpts.

for nia pays big for their art, their fan mail comes ad dressed to
171
N. Y. C.
(CHORUS)
To - mor-row a pent - house
Ww.
Tpt.
that's way up high, to - night the "Y"
Tutti
rall.
why not it's N. Y. C.
Ww.
8va

No. 9

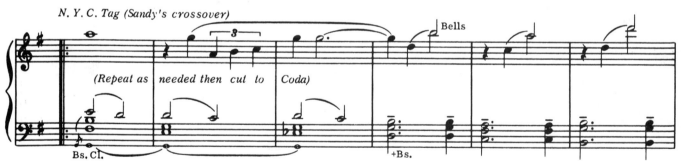

No. 10

EASY STREET

to Eas-y—— Street   when you get there   stay!

56 *Freely*

(dialogue)

Cello

HANNIGAN: "It ain't fair."   ROOSTER:

It ain't

64

HANNIGAN:

fair how we scrounge for three or four bucks—— while she gets War-bucks—— the lit-tle brat!   It ain't

Trpts.

Tbn., Saxs.

+Timp.   *sfz*   *sfz*   Tutti

(87 - 95)

An - nie is the key, yes sir-ee, yes sir - ee, yes sir - ee, yeah!

Tutti

sfz

96 *Dance*

Stgs.

Shuffle rhythm

(99 - 107) 108

110 Trio

Eas - y Street, Eas - y Street.

Trpt.

Tbn.

That's where we're gon - na be. _____

APPLAUSE SEGUE

No. 10a

INTO WARBUCKS' MANSION

fade into telephone conversation

No. 11

YOU WON'T BE AN ORPHAN FOR LONG

76

quits, *(and disappear)*   He'll use his   for - tune   and his   wits. *(so never fear)*

Cross the   street or cross the   sea,   An - nie,   sweet we guar-an - tee   that you

won't   be an   or - phan, no you   won't be   an   or - phan   for   long!

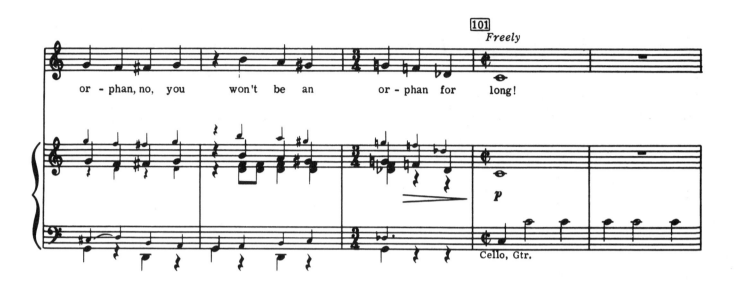

or - phan, no, you won't be an or - phan for long!

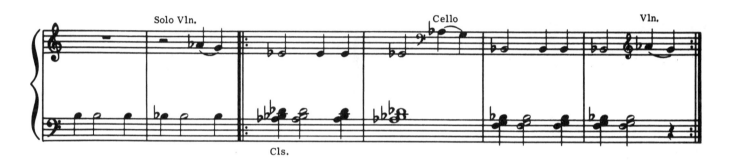

"Meeting your mother and father in a couple of days."

No. 12

ENTRACTE

84

SEGUE AS ONE

No. 12a

OPENING ACT II

No. 13

FULLY DRESSED

16 Your clothes may be Beau Brum-mel-ly, they stand out a mile, but Bro-ther you're

Stgs.

nev-er ful-ly dressed with-out a smile! Who

24 cares what they're wear-ing on Main Street or Sa-ville Row? It's what you

Cls.

wear from ear to ear and not from head to toe, that mat-ters;

rit.

(47-55)   56

Doo doo-dle-oo doo doo doo-dle-oo doo   doo doo doo doo doo doo doo doo   Your   clothes__ may be

Ten. Sax.

Beau Brum-mel-ly,   they stand out a   mile, but broth-er you're nev-er ful-ly dressed, you're nev-er

64

dressed with-out a S - M - I - L - E. Smile, darn ya. Hum _ _ _ _ _

Stgs. 8va

Tbn.

Ten.

fp

Hum _ _ _ _ _

SEGUE AS ONE

No. 14

DRESSED CHILDREN

while, re - mem - ber you're nev - er ful - ly___ dressed with - out a smile.

EASY STREET
REPRISE

MISS HANNIGAN: "Where . . . oh, yeah!"
ROOSTER, LILY, MISS HANNIGAN:

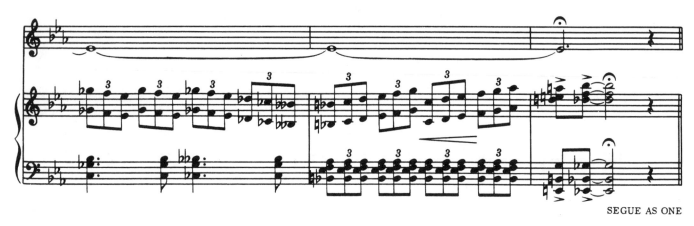

SEGUE AS ONE

No. 16

TRAIN MUSIC

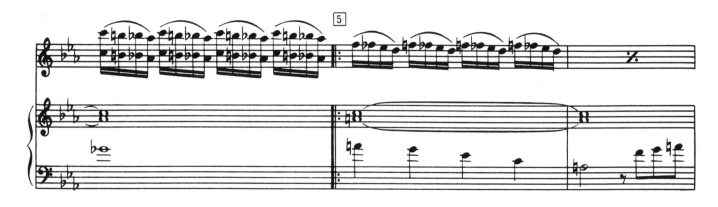

No. 17

CABINET TOMORROW

98

day that's grey and lone-ly,__ I just stick out my chin and grin and say:____ The

sun-'ll come out__ to-mor-row, oh, we got-ta hang on 'til to-mor-row__ come what may!____ To -

mor-row, to-mor-row, I love ya' to-mor-row, you're al-ways a day a-way!__ To -

mor-row, to-mor-row, I love ya to-mor-row, you're on-ly a day

a - way!

No. 18

CABINET END

ANNIE: "Goodbye Mr. President."

Freely (in 2)

No. 19

TRAIN SCENE

Bright (in 4)

No. 20

SOMETHING WAS MISSING

WARBUCKS: "Something else you should know."

Slow Waltz (in 3)   WARBUCKS: 3

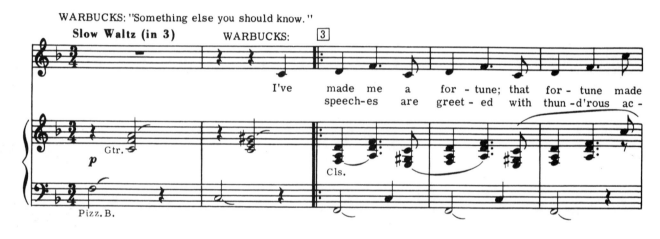

I've made me a for - tune; that for - tune made
speech-es are greet - ed with thun -d'rous ac -

ten. Been head -lined and pro -filed, a - gain and a - gain. But,
claim, at the un - ni - ver-si - ties bear -ing my name. But,

need me for me, Need me for me a - lone? _____

37 *A tempo*

_____ The world was my oy - ster, but where was the pearl? Who

45

dreamed I would find it in one lit - tle girl? Yes, some-thing was

miss - ing, but dreams can come true; that some-thing is no one but

rall

Cello

one lit-tle girl? Yes, some-thing was miss-ing but dreams do come

true; that some-thing is no one but you.

No. 20a

PRE-21

GRACE: "cheese!"

Bright (in 4) TALK

No. 21

I DON'T NEED ANYTHING BUT YOU (Part I)

WARBUCKS:

mouse, I'm rich-er than Mi - das, But noth- ing on earth

could ev - er di - vide us and if to - mor-row I'm an ap - ple sell-er,

too, I don't need an- y - thing but you!

SEGUE AS ONE

SERVANTS' ANNIE (Part II)

No. 21a

PARTY MUSIC

(Out when false parents enter)

No. 21b

SAME EFFECT ON EVERYONE

ROOSEVELT: "I seem to have the same effect
on everyone."

eas- y to tell.____ So may- be I'll for - get how

nice he was to me and how I was al- most his ba - by,

may - be.

Vln.

Gtr.

No. 22

A NEW DEAL FOR CHRISTMAS

18 Bells

ALL:

The snow flakes are fright-ened of fall - ing, and oh, what a fix, ____ no

MOLLY:

pep - per- mint sticks. ___ And all through the land folks are bawl-ing, and filled with de-spair,_'cause

WARBUCKS:

GRACE:

cup-boards are bare. ___ But San - ta's got brand new as - sist- ants, there's noth -ing to

WARBUCKS: 26

fear, they're bring-ing a new deal for Christ-mas, this year!

Cel.+Bells.

Trgl.

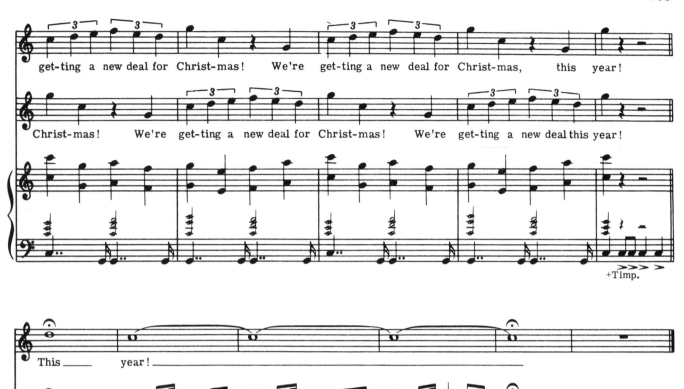

get-ting a new deal for Christ-mas! We're get-ting a new deal for Christ-mas, this year!

Christ-mas! We're get-ting a new deal for Christ-mas! We're get-ting a new deal this year!

This ____ year! _____

ff

rall

+Timp.

No. 23

BOWS

(TOMORROW UTILITY)

Moderato (in 4)

Ⓐ Tutti

Ⓑ

74

f Trpts.
Tbn.,Saxs. *(repeat as needed)*

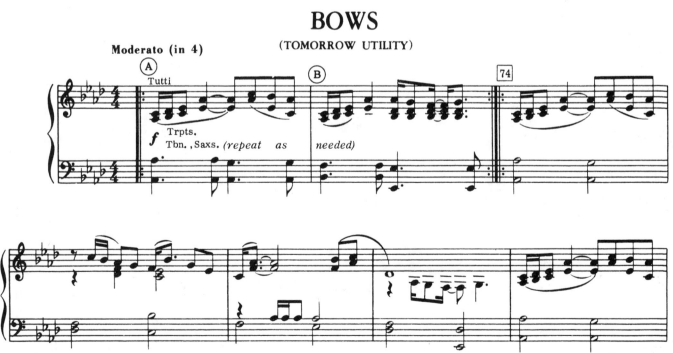

EXIT